TOTALLY HAUNTED UK

CORNWALL

BONNIE GEYER FLOREK

A SPECIAL THANK YOU

To Quade Parker

Thank you for your beautiful art work. Without your willingness to share your talents this special book cover would not have been made possible. I am so grateful to you and I appreciate your fine work. May you be forever successful.

Bonnie Geyer Florek

CONTENTS

ABOUT THE BOOK

The first in a series, *Bonnie Geyer Florek* brings you *Totally Haunted UK.* It is packed full of exciting tales of ghostly sightings and experiences from the most haunted county in the UK, Cornwall.

Impossible to include every story and sighting in this extensive collection the most haunted and unusual encounters have been included. From a variety of Cornwall locations you will read of eerie experiences of people who have visited from around the world.

If you enjoy hearing about exceptionally scary haunts this is the book for you. Once read you will certainly want to experience every single one of these ghostly venues for yourself. If you are planning a trip to Cornwall be sure to take this book along with you.

After reading these stories, you may find yourself planning a trip to Cornwall, even if you hadn't previously planned to visit. Though you may very well want to satisfy your intrigue do be aware that most of these haunted locations are not suitable for the faint of heart.

Happy Haunting !

INTRODUCTION

Cornwall is considered by far to be the most haunted county in the British Isles. With its long history of pirates, ghosts, pixies and other legends, prior skeptics become believers after visiting the area. Paranormal activity abounds in castles, mansions, villages, churches and inns.

The county of Cornwall is situated in the south-west corner of England, UK. It is known not only for its haunts but boasts beautiful beach towns and rugged landscape which overlooks beautiful turquoise waters. Enjoyed in the spring and summer are the beautiful fields of more than one hundred species of wildflowers, where sheep and wild ponies graze right on the edge of high cliffs. Known for its beauty it is enjoyed not only by many of the British, but many from all over the world, as a wonderful vacation area. The beaches attract surfers and sunbathers alike.

There is so much to do in Cornwall besides visiting its beautiful coastal towns, however. Hiking and visiting ruins are also favorite past times. Of course, food is always a good reason to visit anywhere, but Cornwall's Cornish pasties are a real treat. These pockets of pastry or hand pies are filled with meats and vegetables. They are thought to have been originally created for Cornish coal miners who could eat them even with dirty hands, by holding one end of its thick crust. When they were done eating they could just throw the hand-held dirty part away.

THE VILLAGE OF COVERACK

JAMAICA INN

In the heart of Bodmin Moor sits a coaching house built in 1750. It was used as a staging post for changing horses during stagecoach runs over the moor. At one time it was a smuggler's den. Hence its eerie reputation. Jamaica Inn is said to be one of the most haunted locations in England. Residing in the Inn is an evil thief who preys on travelers. He is seen walking through locked doors wearing a tri-corn hat. Room five is said to inhabit a concerned young mother with a baby seen in the mirror. Walking around the courtyard a murdered young smuggler can be seen pacing in the night.

A famous novel was written about the inn by Daphne DuMaurier who lived in the Inn three years prior to writing the book. It was later made into a film by Alfred Hitchcock. It was featured as well in the 1983 television series, 'Jamaica Inn,' starring Jane Seymour. In addition, it is referenced in 'Jamaica Inn,' a song written by Tori Amos on her album The Beekeeper, written while she was travelling by car along the road of the Cornwall cliffs. It was inspired by the legend she had heard of the Inn. Guests and workers at the Inn have witnessed many ghostly sightings.

In the early1900s Jamaica Inn was used as a temperance house. Since then an unexplained presence has been felt, over the years. Recognition has been made on the show Most Haunted, a British paranormal mystery documentary television show. It describes the Inn as one of the spookiest places they have ever investigated. Footsteps can often be heard in the hallways though no one is seen. Horses' hooves and the sound of a carriage's metal rimmed wheels can be heard on dark moonlit nights, right outside the Inn in the courtyard.

There have been reports of a man who suddenly appears just before walking through closed doors. He is wearing a hat and coat. Some even hear a language often considered to be the old Cornish language. Hort and Westcott from the Ghost Society were called in to investigate the Inn. They experienced much paranormal activity mainly in the stable bar, bedroom four, and the smuggler's bar.

Photographs are often sent to the staff of the Inn, as guests have experienced strange incidents during their visits. One recurring and often seen event is that of a murdered sailor. He is seen sitting outside of the building on the wall. Some say he comes back to finish his drink. Reports also often include that of a man hanging from a noose from a tree just outside the Inn.

Because of its name, many have thought that Jamaica Inn was called such because of the smugglers who smuggled rum into the country from Jamaica, storing it at the Inn. Yet the truth is that the Inn was named because of the local Trelawney family of landowners. Two of its family members were Governors of Jamaica in the 18th century.

Though the Inn was built in 1750 it was extended in 1778 to include a coach house, stables and an L-shaped tack room. Smugglers stopped off at the Jamaica Inn, using 100 secret routes to move around their contraband. Later on in years this half-way house was no longer alone on the moor. A church, parsonage, and school were added by Mr. Kodd who owned the land.

The Jamaica Inn was owned, at one time by novelist Alistair MacLean.

Hanging on the wall of the Inn is this picture of a green-cloaked highwayman. He is often seen today in spirit form.

Jamaica Inn
Bolventor
Launceston
Cornwall
PL157TS
Telephone: +44 (0) 1566 86250
Website: www.jamaicainn.co.uk
Email: enquiry@jamaicainn.co.uk

PENGERSICK CASTLE

Pengersick Castle is evidence of five thousand years of history. It is located just inland from the beach at Praa Sands. A four-story tower is the oldest remaining structure and dates back to the sixteenth century. It was part of an extensive fortified Tudor manor belonging to the Pengersick family. The family was known to have committed many murders within the Castle which is why it has such a reputation. Consequently there are many legends that have been passed down over the years. A black robed monk has been seen walking the property at night. Smugglers often unloaded their contraband on the west end of the beach. From there they took it through a tunnel which led to the Castle.

It is said that over 30 spirits have been identified at Pengersick Castle, often called the most haunted location in the UK. Some have refused to stay there as it has been described as frightening and evil. Since the Castle was built in the 12th century, the Pengersick family has lived there. There is evidence however that the site dates back some 5000 years to the Bronze age. The Pengersick family was very well known in Cornwall, where many legends were passed down regarding them. The family suffered in the 1400s during the plague. When the remaining heiress entered a dynastic marriage it resulted in the building of the Tudor Towers which can be seen today at the Castle.

A recent owner of the castle for 35 years, Angela Evans started a trust fund so that the Castle could be maintained long after her death. The castle is now owned by that trust. Restoration is ongoing.

Spirits haunt the grounds and castle, two of whom are murdered monks. Sailors are seen hunting for lost treasure as are a young four year old boy, a demon dog, two prior owners, ghosts from a ship wreck and a holy man from the 14th century. At the end of the medieval garden there is a small forest where one of the monks is usually seen. Though you might expect him to be in traditional monk's robe this particular monk is wearing a wide brimmed hat.

The ghost club has stayed in the Castle many times into the late night. Aired on television, automatic writing which formed a scribbled picture of a woman's face was clearly seen.

Many who stay at the Castle report seeing the apparition of a woman standing looking out of the window, in the late night. After looking out for a time, she turns back and walks to the bed. She clutches her stomach in pain as she lies down. There is no historic record to prove such a thing, but it is believed this could be a prior lady of the house who perhaps was poisoned.

There is a young girl around thirteen years of age who is often seen haunting the battlements. She had been blown over the edge by a strong wind while she was dancing. Since that time she tries to push people over if she does not like them. Women often feel the ghost of a young boy as well, pulling on their dresses or trying to hold their hands.

There are other reports of strange visions in guests' photos: a girl lying on a bed, a woman walking through a wall, unexplained reason for electrical equipment to fail, the ghosts of a cat and dog, and a man swaying in a corner.

The list of sightings at Pengersick Castle is extensive. When a douser named Ron Kirby doused with water one of the bedrooms he found 28 presences of spirits dating from 1500 to 1814. A demon dog with red eyes called a 'devil dog' is often seen by the fireplace in one of the bedrooms. Believed to be the ghost of Engrina of Pengersick she appears in white, in one of the bedrooms. The ghosts of several sailors are seen wandering the grounds. When ships were wrecked in Cornwall surviving sailors were murdered. Many ghostly sailors are spotted in the area. Voices can be heard coming from unconsecrated land where they can be heard calling out into the night. It has been said that one of the rooms has a trapped demon in it. Floating lights or orbs are also seen.

There are many paranormal reports made concerning Pengersick Castle. Regular investigations are held at that location.

Pengersick Castle
Pengersick Lane
Praa Sands, Penzance, TR20 9SJ
Telephone: +44 (0) 1872 260 699
Website: www.pengersickcastle.com
Email: info@pengersickcastle.org.uk

BODMIN MOOR / BODMIN JAIL

BODMIN MOOR

Bodmin Moor is full of myths and legends. The ghost of Tregeagle was the 17th century magistrate under the Duchy of Cornwall. He can be heard at Dozmary Pool, howling across the moors where King Arthur's sword is believed to remain. Murdered by her crippled lover, Charlotte Dymond's ghost is seen on the slopes of Roughtor wearing a gown and a silk bonnet. There is strong evidence of a huge, black, panther-like cat. Called the Beast of Bodmin Moor it has been seen over sixty times. The Beast is given to savaging livestock in the late night hours.

BODMIN JAIL

Bodmin Jail (Bodmin Gaol) was designed by Sir John Call, built in 1779 and closed in 1927. Since that time there has been no prison in the county of Cornwall. It was the first British prison to house prisoners in individual cells. The Debtors Act of 1869 ended imprisonment for debt. Consequently the extra space came to be used by the Admiralty for naval prisoners. During World War I some of Britain's priceless national treasures were kept in the jail, including Domesday Book and the Crown Jewels of the United Kingdom. The first hanging took place in 1785 before the jail was even completely built. The last hanging was held in 1909 after which future hangings were carried out in Exeter Prison. Most of the buildings are now in ruins though parts of the prison are now a tourist attraction. It is an former historic prison on the edge of Bodmin Moor. It is known for its famously well-attended public hangings which took place until 1862. Today the jail is a museum which tells of the grisly crimes and sentences that took place. Bodmin jail exudes its eerie past even from a distance. Underground passages still exist.

For King George III in 1779, prisoners brought in 20,000 tons of granite and built the jail. The granite was taken from Bodmin's now called 'Cuckoo Quarry.' It has been said that the jail once held the crown jewels.

During very dark times this place of punishment held over 150 prisoners of which 55 were hanged. In 1844 William and James Lightfoot were hanged, convicted for the robbery and murder of well-known Neville Norway, a timber merchant.

Twenty thousand gathered to watch the executions. One of them is since reportedly seen in one of the ground floor jail cells. In 1909 William Hampton was hanged. This was the very last hanging at this site. It was performed in private with just one of the prison staff present, the Governor, the High Sheriff, Mayor, and local Vicar.

There was much suffering and many deaths at the Bodmin Jail. Consequently there have been great numbers of paranormal occurrences within its walls. Due to the terrible conditions the prisoners endured many died here.

Wandering around the jail is Matthew Week's ghost. He pleads his innocence still today. Selina Wedge, who was hanged for murder of her illegitimate son, is also often seen. She tries to take young children who are visiting the jail and quells her feeling on pregnant women.

Anne Jefferies roams around the jail still today, having been left to starve to death. She was accused of being a witch and refused to admit it. It took three months for her to die, which made many believe she did indeed have supernatural powers.

The figure of a priest is seen near the chapel. Seen in the bar / restaurant area today are ghostly apparitions. Mediums have contacted many spirits, one being a prostitute executed wrongly. Naval officers were housed in the area where a lean and haggard looking man is still seen in one of the cells.

A feeling of being watched, many visitors have seen orbs down the halls of the jail and have heard keys rattling, voices and footsteps. They also experience a feeling of being touched and a tugging at their clothes. Children can be heard screaming in the ground floor cells. Stones have been thrown at the current owners in the naval area, and loud bangs are heard coming from the empty jail by those who stand outside.

Bodmin Jail
Berrycoombe Road
Bodmin
PL31 2NR
UK
Telephone: +44 1208 76292
Website: www.bodminjail.org
Email: info@bodminjail.org

Bodmin Jail

Sir John Call, 1779 Oil Painting

TRIPPET STONES / STRIPPEL STONES / THE CHEESEWRING

TRIPPET STONES / STRIPPEL STONES

The ancient sites of the Trippet Stones, Stripple Stones and the unusual King Arthur's Hall date back to the early Bronze Age and have no connection to King Arthur. They are located in a large area of commons and downs. Together these 56 upright stones and mounds form a rectangle.

It once consisted of 26 stones yet only 11 remain today. The circular nature of the site is most unusual for Cornwall.

The Stripple Stones form a henge rather than a typical stone circle. They are situated in a way that is representative of some sort of astronomical or calendaring function.

To the north of the moor are the villages of St Breward, Blisland and Altarnun. Though pretty, they are all very different from the typical Cornish fishing villages on the coast. Blisland is built around a village green which makes it very unusual for Cornwall. Interestingly, the parish church stands on one side of the green and the village pub stands on the other side. Very pretty cottages envelop the area as they scatter around the village green.

A bit larger than Blisland, St. Breward is where the highest church in Cornwall stands. Largely defined by its surroundings, the area is quite lovely on its own.

On the outer eastern area of the moor is the village of Altarnum. In the valley of Penpont Water cottages line the main street where water flows down the side trenches. At the bottom of the hill is the River Inney where the church of St Nonny is located. It is also known as 'the Cathedral of the Moor', with its high tower. An ancient packhorse bridge crosses the river.

To the south of the moor there is an open area known for its legends and ghost stories. They are related to the Jamaica Inn in Bolventor. Daphne du Maurier's novel about smugglers, 'Jamaica Inn' made this area famous. Down the road just a few miles is Dozmary Pool which holds great mystery. It is known as the lake where King Arthur's sword, Excalibur was thrown after his death. 'Lady of the Lake' is said to have caught it.

The Trippet Stones
Blisland, North Cornwall

THE CHEESEWRING

As in the northern moor, remains of many settlements of the Bronze Age still remain. Much of the remains can be seen in Craddock Moor and

Stowe's Hill near the village of Minions. Hut circles and stones form a stone row and four circles of stone. Together they are known as the Hurlers. It is often stated and believed that these are people who turned to stone for not observing the Sabbath, instead playing a game of hurling ball. The site is among the old South Phoenix mine representing two millennia of history.

Stowe's Hill overlooks Minions which is above Stowe's Pound, a hilltop enclosure from the Stone Age. Though some of the hillside has been worn away by the now flooded granite quarry, it is most beautiful to see in the Cheesewring. This odd pile of rocks stands 12 feet tall and is completely natural. Because of the many years of wind and rain erosion, a pile of granite discs look like a cider press called by the same name.

At the site of Daniel Gumb's cave, Stowe's hill sits nearby. Not wanting to pay rent, Mr. Gumb, a stone cutter mined into the side of Stowe's hill to create a personal dwelling.

He actually created three rooms, raising 9 children living also with 3 different wives. After teaching himself mathematics he carved the Euclid theorem into one of the stones of the house.

It is said that the Cheesewring is the result of a contest between a man and a giant. Christianity had just been brought to the British Islands when the giants who lived at the top of the mountains were not happy about it. The saints had invaded their land and were declaring their wells as sacred. One of the larger giants, Uther was given the task of ridding their land of the saints. He confronted the frail Saint Tue who proposed a rock throwing contest. If Uther won the saints would leave Cornwall. If Saint Tue won then the giants would convert to Christianity. Uther took his turn first and easily threw a small rock to the top of nearby Stowe's Hill. Tue prayed for assistance and picking up a huge slab found it was very light. One after the other they threw their rocks, stacking them up in perfect piles. When the score was twelve stones each, Uther threw a thirteenth stone but it rolled down the hill. Tue picked up this fallen stone and as he lifted it, an angel appeared to carry it to the top of the pile of rocks. Seeing this, Uther conceded and most of the giants decided to follow Christianity after that.

To get there:

Cheesewring is situated on the eastern side of Bodmin Moor on Stowe's Hill in the parish of Linkinhorne about four miles north of Liskeard

Take the A30 road towards St. Breward not far from Jamaica Inn. The Trippett Stones can be seen from the road. The Stripple Stones are about ½ mile farther in the ENE direction.

The easiest way to find the stones from the East is to watch the two-way road. The turn off is the first on the right immediately after the road ends, once you've passed the Jamaica Inn.

Once on the side road, continue to a crossroads (the first intersection on the road). Turn right to Hawks Tor Farm. The stones will be off to the left of this area about halfway between the intersection and the farm.

DOZMARY POOL

Dozmary Pool is surrounded by an empty wilderness known as Bodmin Moor. The home of Lady of the Lake it is said that King Arthur rowed out to receive the sword Excalibur from Lady of the Lake, who had made Dozmary Pool her home.

It is said that Sir Bedivere brought the dying King Arthur back to the banks of the pool. The king instructed him to cast Excalibur into Dozmary Pool, from whence it came.

As hard as he might, Sir Bedivere could not bring himself to cast the beautiful sword into the water. He went back to the King not once but twice, telling him of the difficulty he was having following his orders.

On his third return to the King however, the loyal knight had reluctantly complied with Arthur's wishes. When questioned, according to Tennyson, Sir Bedivere was able to reply:

"… With both hands I flung him, wheeling him;

But when I looked again, behold an arm,

Clothed in white samite, mystic, wonderful,

That caught him by the hilt,

and brandish'd him three times,

and drew him under in the mere..."

Around the area of Dozmary Pool stand celtic crosses that can hardly stand, after so many years. Mysterious stone circles remain nearby. Old abandoned mine buildings still remain in their run-down state, bearly able to hold themselves up.

That same area claims to be the hunting grounds of the Beast of Bodmin. Reports of sightings have been made over the years, regarding a black panther-like cat and mutilated livestock.

There is a legend of a man named Jan Tregeagle whose spirit sits quietly on the banks of Dozmary Pool. A dark spirit, his despairing cries are heard clearly into the night. It is said that he has been doomed to eternal torment due to the evil acts he committed in life. He was a magistrate who lived in the early 1600s.

Because of his less than reputable ways, a clergyman had to be bribed to allow Tregeagle's body to be buried on the grounds of St. Breock's churchyard, upon his death.

Not long after his death however, there were two families from Bodmin who were in a dispute. One had hired Jan Tregeagle as their lawyer. He had defrauded them out of ownership of their own land after forging documents to make it appear that he was the rightful owner of the disputed land.

When the judge was ready to rule, the defendant asked if he could bring in one final witness. At that moment, the air in the courtroom turned cold as a strong and howling wind blew through the courtroom. Suddenly the spirit of Mr. Tregeagle was standing in the witness box. Under oath, his spirit was forced to admit his wrong doing, at which time there was a unanimous verdict in the rightful owner's favor.

Jan Tregeagle

With the clergy's help, an attempt was made to save Tregeagle's troubled soul. He was given a task in attempt to keep him busy for the rest of eternity. Taken to the banks of Dozmary Pool he was condemned to empty the pool completely with a perforated limpet shell.

To see to it that he kept on task, a pack of headless demon hounds were summoned to harm him should he ever break from the tedious task. Still today, Tregeagle's screams of rage can be heard at Dozmary Pool.

Dozmary Pool on Bodmin Moor
To get there:
The pool is reached off a minor road from the A30 near the Jamaica Inn from Bolventor.

KINGS HEAD

The Kings Head has been known by several names, over the years. Built back in 1623 it has been called The Indian Queen in 1773, The London Inn in 1785, and The Five Lanes Inn in 1795. Once a staging post for coaches it was also a meeting place for Cavaliers and Roundheads during the Civil War of 1642.

A former landlady, Peggy Bray's ghost haunts the Kings Head pub today. Her ghost is most often heard walking the long corridor. Many think she is walking around the building to see that it is being run the way she always ran it. Some report feeling a chill near the doorway about half way down the hallway.

King's Head
Five Lanes, Altarnun, Launceston, PL15 7RX
Telephone: 01566 86241
Website: www.thekingshead-hotel.co.uk

THE THREE PILCHARDS

The first pub built in Polperro, it is thought to have been given its name after three pilchard curers. They often brought their fish to the pub for tasting.

Today there is a ghost haunting the pub. It is often thought to be one of the members of a family who lived there in the 1800s. Ennis Jones reports often seeing the ghosts when she owned The Three Pilchards a while back.

A local newspaper, The Cornish Times published an article regarding the ghosts she had seen. Ennis reports that she often saw a woman upstairs in the pub when she was just a girl. Later in years, after moving back with her husband Alan Jones, he also saw the ghosts and heard noises.

Researching the pub and its past, Andy Jones found some old records regarding the family who lived there from 1856-1870. While the mother had often been beaten by the father, one of their children would try to stop him from the beatings. The noise that is now heard in the pub is that of one of those scuffles.

Several of the pub regulars report seeing the ghosts. One even reports having seen a woman milking a cow in the back yard.

There is also an unexpected smell in the pub. Though none are present, the smell of violets hovers in the air for no reason. It leaves just as quickly as it came.

The Three Pilchards
Address: The Quay, Polperro, PL13 2QZ
Telephone: 01503 272233
Website: www.threpilchardspolperro.co.uk

CRUMPLEHORN INN

Part of a complex, the Crumplehorn Inn was once a small settlement and corn mills. It has been a pub since 1972.

There are many sightings and reported hauntings from visitors and overnight guests alike. Some are spotted in the public areas of the Inn and some in its private rooms.

Visitors report seeing something moving out of the corner of their eye, disappearing soon afterward. Others say they hear doors opening. Guests also report seeing a ghost in one of the bedrooms with his hand on his head.

Past owners have also reported hearing spirits. Voices and whispers are heard in the night from the loft above, though the loft cannot be accessed. The voice is believed to be that of a First World War soldier who had left the army and is still hiding in that loft. The female voice also heard is believed to be his lover.

Like so many of these haunted locations, The Crumplehorn Inn was investigated several times. In November 2004 one investigative group reported hearing a cup moving in the kitchen. They also found a light that had been turned off and an odd shadow could be seen in one of their videos.

Crumplehorn Inn
Address: Polperro, Cornwall. PL13 2RJ
Telephone: 01503 272348
Website: www.crumplehorn-inn.co.uk

BOCHYM MANOR

    In the village of Cury stands Bochym Manor. Stephen and Richard Davey were thrill-seekers. They were involved in the development of Cornish mines during the boom period. They purchased an ancient manor house and estate at

Bochym. Richard's nephew and Stephen's son, Joshua Sydney Davey (1842-1909), later inherited the estate.

Today it is residence to two ghosts. One is called the 'short pink lady' and the other stands at one of the bedroom windows looking out at whomever might be standing and watching.

Location: Near Helston in West Cornwall

TRERICE MANOR

Nestled peacefully at the end of a winding road Trerice Manor sets on a secluded spot in a sheltered valley. It was built in 1573 by Sir John Arundell.

Because the Arundells were faithful Royalists their fortunes suffered a loss during Cromwell's Protectorship during the Civil War.

As the Restoration of the Monarchy came about in 1660, their estates turned back to what they had once been.

By the 18th century they were not spending as much time at their Cornish retreat. Consequently, in 1802 their 400 year occupancy ended. It was then passed on to the Acland family.

The Aclands began restoring the property's great chamber. Today it is the most beautiful part of the manor, boasting a beautiful barrel ceiling. As the sunlight shines through the 576 panes of glass one is reminded of the glory of this 16th century east window.

In 1915 having been in residence for 113 years, the family sold it. At that time hints of ghostly inhabitants were beginning to be realized.

The ages old story tells of 'wicked lord Arundell' who seduced a young servant girl and cruelly discarded her when she became pregnant. The girl later committed suicide. Her ghost is said to be lingering in the manor still today. Though she is never seen it is clear that she enters the room when the temperature suddenly drops and the smell of lilac fills the air.

Her presence is felt passing by guests and visitors. Several have reported hearing the rustle of her skirt as she goes by.

Many feel that the library has an eerie feel to it. Some believe the spirit of the young servant girl spends much of her time in that room. Some visitors have been known to wait a bit before entering the room as they can feel her presence beforehand.

Perhaps she is the 'Grey Lady' whose stately form is often seen drifting around the house's gallery. Or perhaps she is another entity who makes the inexplicable bumping sounds and other noises throughout the building, at various times of the day and night.

Trerice Manor inhabits yet another ghost of a stable boy. His spirit appears near the courtyard and stables. It is said that he was killed when the horses were suddenly frightened and trampled him to death.

Trerice Manor
Kestle Mill
Newquay
Cornwall
TR8 4PG
Telephone: +44 01637 875404
Directions---The nearest major road is A3058. Turn at Kestle Mill on Newquay to St. Austell Road. Trerice is one mile up the road.

COTEHELE HOUSE

Cotehele House is located along the beautiful riverside. It was constructed between 1485 and 1687. It has not changed much over the years, standing amidst a most intimate setting.

For many centuries The Edgcumbe family owned the home. Built of solid stone it is representative of the family's status of wealth and the expensive taste of the elite. Within its stone walls the finest of tapestries hang as well as beautiful art work. The stair case is worn as you make your way up to the large bedrooms, four post beds included.

Many spirits have passed through its rooms which gives the house a strong feeling of mystery. Some report the smell of an herbal fragrance throughout the house along with the sound of sad music. A cloud of spirit forms are often seen making their way through the house.

Servants have reported seeing the spirit of a girl in a white dress seen over and over in certain rooms. No one knows who she might be. Some who know nothing about this spirit report seeing her, not realizing it is not a living being. When they ask staff who she is, 'the girl with the long hair in a white, flimsy dress,' it is realized that she is indeed a ghost. Some of the staff do not let on, just shrugging and saying 'Don't worry, you must have seen a ghost.'

Cotehele House
Address: St. Domimick, Saltash, PL12 6TA
Telephone: +44 1579 351346
Website: www.nationaltrust.org.uk/cotehele
Email: cotehele@nationaltrust.org.uk

ST BARTHOLOMEW'S CHURCH

Warleggan Town Sign

In the little village of Warleggan stands St. Bartholomew's Church. This remote Cornish village has a spooky feel about it.

As you see "twinned with Narnia" clearly imprinted on the village sign you will sense a feeling of great unease.

Inside the little church of St. Bartholomew there is a photograph of a past vicar named F.W. Densham. He was known to be eccentric, his fame extending beyond church boundaries.

The Reverend F.W. Densham arrived in the remote village of Warleggan in 1931. A heavy-set man with a square jaw, he was sixty-one years old at the time. He was very set in his ways and had done much traveling prior to that time.

Wanting things to always go his way, he had alienated his parishioners within just one year of his arrival. They contacted the Bishop of Truro, wanting the Reverend Densham to be removed immediately. When nothing changed, they refused to attend his services though he continued to preach each Sunday, to an empty church building. They say he would set cardboard cut-outs in the pews, writing the names of past vicars on each one. At the end of each service he would write in the church register 'No fog, no wind, no rain, no congregation.'

When news of the situation got out to other areas the Reverend became a kind of celebrity. By the 1950s his congregation became a slew of reporters not only from the UK but as far away as the American weekly *Life*.

He died a very lonely man in 1953. His death came to him on the staircase of the vicarage. When his body was found two days later, his arm was outstretched trying to reach the bell rope. Though he needed his unhappy parishioners to respond to him, it is unlikely that they would have helped him had he actually been able to ring that bell.

Since his death, his ghost is often seen walking the now overgrown path leading to the vicarage. Though he is known for being less than a vicar should have been, the intrigue of it all still brings visitors to the old desolate church. The old Visitors Book still remains where one particular comment gets much attention. "No fog, no wind, no rain....No sign of the vicar!"

Directions: Take A39 to Station Road. Travel about 4 miles and turn right to Warleggan.

THE ST KEW INN

One of the few buildings in the little village of St. Kew, The St Kew Inn was the first licensed in the 18th Century. The building however, dates back to the 1600s.

Under the slate floor in the huge kitchen one section causes great mystery to many. It is that area where the skeleton of a teenage girl was uncovered in the 1970s by workmen doing some repairs. After scientifically investigating it was determined that the remains had been there for nearly 100 years. No one knew who she was however, nor did they know any stories surrounding the building that would give reason for such a burial.

She was later given a proper burial in consecrated ground. Her prior burial place was covered with concrete. Her spirit remains in the St. Kew Inn, however. Those who work there now call her 'Adele.' She only appears when workmen make further alterations to the property. When this happens, a cold sensation is felt as her invisible ghost passes by.

Sometimes her full spectral apparition is seen. Adele sadly and silently passes by, her eyes wide open as if looking toward a specific goal in the distance. Most are not afraid of her as she is now recognized as the Inn's oldest resident.

St. Kew Inn
Bodmin, Cornwall PL30 3HB
Telephone:01208 841259
Website: www.stkewinn.co.uk
Email: info@stkewinn.co.uk

THE HEADLAND HOTEL

In Newquay, The Headland Hotel sits at the southern end of Fistral Beach. It's eerie façade was featured in Roald Dahl's *The Witches*. The hotel has hosted Royals including Edward VII and Prince Charles as well as many celebrities.

The Hotel is known for its many ghostly residents seen floating silently down the halls. Some such ghosts are those of men in uniform. It is thought that they are servicemen who were there when it was a military hospital during World War II. One of their nurses still tries to take care of those who are alive today. Touching the cheeks of sleeping guests she attempts to awaken them.

There is the ghost of a maid who is seen disappearing through a wall in the ladies' powder room. There used to be a door at the site where her body leaves the room.

The Headland Hotel
Fistral, Newquay,
Cornwall TR7 1EW
Telephone: +44 (0) 1637 872211
Website: www.headlandhotel.co.uk
Email: reservations@headlandhotel.co.uk

THE DOLPHIN TAVERN

The Dolphin Tavern is very old. Made of heavy granite it is situated in Penzance where the views over the sea are breathtaking. It is possible to see all the way out to St. Michael's Mount. The Tavern was used by John Hawkins in the 1580s as a place to recruit Cornish sailors to join the Navy to defend England against the Spanish Armada. Sir Walter Raleigh who was Hawkin's fellow sea dog, is said to have smoked the first pipe of tobacco on English soil.

Once used as a courtroom, the Dolphin Inn has at least three ghosts. 'George' is thought to have been a captain of a ship. He seems to be dressed quite fashionably, tri-corn hat and frock coatincluded. Of course the coat is decorated with brass buttons, and lace ruffles hang from the neck and sleeves. After being seen walking in the corridors and upstairs rooms he suddenly disappears.

A lady from the Victorian era is often seen passing by surprised drinkers in the main bar. Recently while one of the staff was waiting for the Inn to open for lunch, she materialized coming from the wall he was standing beside. She hovered across to the other side of the room before vanishing through the wall.

A third ghost is that of a young light-haired man. Overnight guests have reported seeing him upon their awakening. He is either standing beside them or sitting on the foot of the bed. Some guests have been known to talk to him as he melts away.

More recently, an old sea captain dressed in hat and ruffles is heard paying guests a most surprising visit. It is thought that he may be a victim of the famous 'Hanging Judge,' Judge Jeffries (1648-89). A series of trials were once held in what is now the dining room, which may explain this sighting. Perhaps it is the ghost of an old smuggler attempting to reclaim his casks of brandy which were found during the renovations in the cellar.

The Dolphin Tavern
Quay Street
Penzance, Cornwall TR18 4BD
Telephone: 01736 364106
Website: www.dolphintavern.co.uk
Email: dolphintavern@tiscali.co.uk

PUNCH BOWL INN

The tale of an angry old rector falling to his death is often associated with the Punch Bowl Inn. It is believed that his angry soul inhabits a demonic black cockerel. While fetching a bottle of wine in the cellar the old rector fell to his death.

The night that this happened he was having dinner with his assistant who had fallen in love with the rector's young wife. Some seem to feel that he was perhaps pushed down those stairs. The very next day is when the black cockerel suddenly appeared, attacking everyone nearby. The bird flew angrily through the window of the Punch Bowl Inn to an old oven. One of the kitchen maids imprisoned him inside of it. A mason was immediately called to cement the angry bird inside.

The Punch Bowl and Ladle
Penelewey, Feock,
Truro, TR3 6QY
Telephone: 01872 862237
Website: www.punchbowlandladle.com
Email: enquiries@punchbowlandladle.com

CHARLOTTE DYMOND

Found murdered on the slopes of Roughtor was Charlotte Dymond. Dead since Sunday April 14th, 1844 she is since known as one of Cornwall's most famous ghosts. She had a crippled lover who worked as a farmhand. Called Matthew Weeks, he was later hanged at Bodmin Gaol for his crime. No one is certain that he was the murderer, however. On the anniversary of her death Charlotte is seen in a gown, red shawl and silk bonnet, walking the grounds.

A memorial stone has been placed on the site of her murder and the story has been immortalized in 'The Ballad of Charlotte Dymond,' by Cornish poet Charles Causley.

Near the car park at Roughtor stands a memorial to Charlotte. Often visited today, flowers continue to be laid in her memory.

Rough Tor / Roughtor
St. Breward
North Cornwall

DUPWORTH MANOR

In Dupworth stands a very old manor house. Haunted by the ghost of a nun affectionately called 'Flo,' she has been heard striking matches and opening the lock on the cabinet in the drawing room.

Even since the manor was demolished and the sight has become Duporth Holiday Village, 'Flo' has not left that spot. The spinning roundabout in the playground spins seemingly on its own, despite there is no breeze or blowing wind. A sewing machine sews without anyone present and a kettle boils with no one in sight, from a locked and unattended room. One time the sewing machine stopped when someone yelled 'no thanks Flo - I don't need you today.'

Near the old farmhouse, many report feeling a presence. A young 5 year old girl was heard talking with someone on the landing one day. Her elderly grandmother could not see anyone. The little girl reported talking with a nice old lady in a black dress.

Location: Duporth is within the outskirts of St. Austell near Charlestown within the southwest of Cornwall.

THE LEGEND OF BLACKWAYS COVE

Known to be haunted, Blackways Cove sets on an isolated inlet. The spirits may very well be the ghosts of shipwrecked sailors who drowned as their vessels were torn to shreds by nearby rocks.

Another theory seems more likely, that of the spirit of a man haunting the scene of his crime. There was a man who had two sons. They all farmed the area together. Upon his death, the estate was left to his eldest son, leaving his brother with absolutely no inheritance. Upset, the younger son seethed with jealousy that became so crippling that he set out to act on his anger and to seek revenge. He quietly snuck onto the property of the farm one night and set fire to the buildings. The entire area was completely burned to the ground. The ruins can still be seen near Blackways. Of the farmhouse and outbuildings just a few stones remain. The very next day, after everything burned to the ground, the jealous brother found out that his brother had died the day before leaving him the entire estate.

Location: Blackways Cove is an isolated inlet along the coast from the golden North Cornwall beach of Trebarwith Strand

THE TALLAND GHOST HUNTER

On Cornwall's East coast not far from the fishing villages of Looe and Polperro, there is a little village called Talland. The town vicar, Parson Richard Dodge pastored the church between 1713 and 1747. He was known for being a ghost hunter and exorcist which was a convenient cover-up for his illegal smuggling activities. Dodge told his parishioners that he could drive away the Devil, saying he had even met the Devil driving a sable coach drawn by two headless horses. To be certain that these God-fearing people would stay away from the area where the smuggling took place at night, he told them of demons on nearby Bridle Lane, a path that leads down to the beach where he took part in illegal activities.

To boost his reputation of fear, he told his parishioners that as he approached, evil spirits would cry out 'Dodge is come! I must be gone!' His supposed power to stop evil was known by people all over the county. It is also said that the original church building was to be built in nearby Pulpit. After the construction began, each morning brought the same situation. The stones laid the day before were moved to the present site of the church today. A scary voice was heard saying 'if you would my wish fulfill build the church on Talland Hill.' As the builders were quite superstitious they took orders and built the church where it stands today.

Location: On Cornwall's east coast, not far from the villages of Looe and Polperro

THE PHANTOM COACH

A man by the name of Cliff Hocking often took rides through the quiet roads of Mevagissey. One wet November afternoon he was met by something that would startle him beyond belief.

On his way to Truro to visit his ailing wife in the hospital, he was suddenly met head on by an old fashioned stagecoach with four horses leading. The coachman wore a large coat with wide blue lapels. He was whipping the horses to keep them running at record speed, blowing a posthorn. Terrified, Mr. Hocking slammed on his brakes. Holding his hands over his eyes he sat still in his stalled car awaiting what he knew would be a complete disaster. He could hear the thundering wheels, galloping hooves and blast of the horn getting louder and louder. As it was about to crash into him the sound suddenly and abruptly stopped.

Expecting to see something when he uncovered his eyes he was shocked to find nothing in sight.

The scene just read is not uncommon. There have been many reports of phantom coaches with ghostly horses leading them along, especially in the very haunted county of Cornwall.

Mr. Hocking still remembers that the coach was bright red, low to the ground, had small doors and windows and a sloping rear. This type of coach would have been used to carry mail to villages and towns about two hundred years ago. The thought is that perhaps the coachman was running late for his mail run, that day, or had a secret that he didn't want anyone seeing him involved in. Walter Cross of Mevagissey, had introduced the stagecoach service to Cornwall in 1796. He was a known smuggler. Perhaps he was the one on the coach that day.

Mevagissey Information Center
Mevagissey, Cornwall PL26 6U
Telephone: 01726 844857
Website: www.mevagissey-cornwall.co.uk

THE GHOST SHIP OF CHYGWIDDEN

There was an heir of the Chygwidden estate who had left some years before. He returned by ship with a dark skinned companion some years later. This man he brought back with him was as intriguing as well as odd. He rarely spoke to anyone except 'The Captain' as the heir had been called by the townspeople.

Their relationship was less than normal as they fought all the time. No one else was allowed to get involved with any of it. 'The Captain' seemed to be edgy since his return, as he was drinking quite heavily. His dying wish was to be buried at sea before he had taken his last breath. He died before anyone could follow through with his final wish however.

'The Captain's' companion left with his dog soon afterward by boat. The lady of the house also departed. None of them was seen alive ever again. However, since that time there have been many sightings reported of a ship believed to be the one 'The Captain' wished to die in. It is spotted as a mist moving back over the land to Chygwidden.

Chygwidden
Kenwyn, Cornwall
Telephone: 01872 322162
Email: countyfarms@cornwall.gov.uk

CHAPEL STREET - PENZANCE

Chapel Street is lined with history. From its old buildings come many old interesting stories. The oldest street in Penzance, it also boasts four pubs. Inside The Union Hotel is where the 1791 remains of the oldest Georgian theatre in the country still stands, as does the town's original assembly room. One of the oldest buildings in Penzance is The Regent. It is the site of a former temperance hall which is four hundred years old. The Turk's Head, the oldest pub in Penzance was named after a famous admiral of the seventeenth century. It is decorated with figureheads and cannons brought up by divers from local wrecks. The figure of a smuggler with a gun can be seen lying on the roof.

About 50 years ago, the building on Chapel Street which is now used as a medical office was once a mansion. The mansion was owned by an old woman named Mrs. Baines. Behind the mansion was a large orchard and garden alongside Vounderveor Lane. All around was an open field where there were no homes. Mrs. Baines was proud of her many fruit trees. Boys from town would steal the fruit as it was most delicious. This often happened when the old lady and her serving man John would watch the gardens in the late night and early morning. One night, not sure that John was watching carefully, Mrs. Baines went to find him. Since she could not, she went to one of her apple trees and shook it, fruit falling to the ground. She wanted to show John that she knew he was not there, since fruit had been 'stolen.'

Unfortunately for Mrs. Baines John was nearby holding a firearm, sleeping under a bush. He had heard the rustling of the tree, woke up and not knowing who it was, shot her. As she fell to the ground John was quite afraid. He ran away but was found days later in the Castle an Dinas nearly starved to death.

When he had fired at Mrs. Baines her back had been to him so the shot had mostly hurt her lower body. Dr. Giddy performed surgery. Not long afterward the old lady died. She continued to watch over her orchard after dark, haunting the property. At times she was seen under the tree where she had been shot.

Mrs. Baines did not stay on her own property however. Her spirit was haunting other areas of the garden and was seen day and night. She was such a nuisance that no one wanted to live in the house. She'd walk from room to room slamming doors, moving furniture and would sometimes make the sound of clanging dishes.

People in the street could hear her even when no one was in the house. Her spirit was often seen as an apparition through the windows. Lights were seen coming from the parlors and bedrooms as on-lookers stood on Chapel Street.

The owners hired an exorcist perhaps by the name of Singleton, to go to the house to calm the spirit and send it on its way. He was successful as he got her spirit down to the banks on western green. He bound her there for a thousand years. She has not been heard from ever since.

Chapel Street
Penzance, TR18 4AP

PENDENNIS CASTLE

Built by Henry VIII Pendennis Castle sits just outside Falmouth. It was meant to protect the Carrick Roads from invasion by France and Spain. In 1646 there was a famous siege that took place. The Royalists were trapped inside for six months. For survival they were forced to eat their horses and dogs. They finally surrendered.

Other ghostly occurrences are also experienced at this site. Special tours are given of some areas of the castle that are not often open to the public, including the underground kitchen. Because of ghosts and odd occurrences this part of the castle is usually closed off.

Still heard within the walls of the castle are the piercing screams of a kitchen maid. She had fallen and died while carrying a tray of food, perhaps pushed to her death. Strange footsteps are still heard by many visitors. They come from a staircase that no longer leads anywhere.

There is a portrait of the governor of the castle on the first floor. His very friendly presence is felt. He did love the castle so his spirit remains. His presence does not bring fear.

A ghost remains where the ammunition was kept. Though no one has been given a key to that area he is often seen there.

Castle Close
Falmouth, TR11 4LP
Telephone: +44 1326 316594
Website: www.pendenniscastle.com
Email: info@pendenniscastle.com

TINTAGEL CASTLE

     The ruins of a twelfth century castle, Tintagel is associated with King Arthur. There are at least five well-known ghosts who reside there. Three of them remain at the Camelot Castle Hotel. They not only throw paintings from the walls, they also awaken people from a deep sleep to give them a bed bath. They are known to go through hotel bins as well. One of the ghosts is a past employee of the hotel. He died about seventy years ago quite suddenly. He is still seen walking along the path to the hotel from his cottage, once owned by Kate Winslet. Beneath the castle remains a dark, damp cave. It is believed to be haunted by Merlin.

Castle Road
Tintagel,PL34 0HE
Telephone: +44 1840 770328
Website: www.tintagelcastle.co.uk

PRIDEAUX PLACE

An Elizabethan manor house, Prideaux Place sits near Padstow. Since its completion in 1592 it has been owned by the Prideaux-Brune family. Paranormal activity is often heard and reported.

There is a scullery boy whose ghost is seen running around the kitchen. A woman dressed in nineteenth century clothing sits and sews in the morning room. Honor Fortescue's ghost is often seen as well. She was the wife of Humphrey Prideaux. Since his death she is seen in a green dress chasing people out of the bedrooms. She is known to have thrown herself off the upper balcony falling to her death, after her husband died.

Prideaux Place
Padstow PL28 8RP
Telephone: +44 1841 532411
Website: http://www.prideauxplace.co.uk
Email: office@prideauxplace.*co*.uk.

WHEAL COATES

All the way down to the sea goes the mine at Wheal Coates near St Agnes. Through the grate in the floor of the Towanroath engine house, it can be heard crashing against the rocks.

The ruined engine house is said to be the most famous industrial building in Cornwall. The mine shaft can be accessed through a large cave at the far end of Chapel Porth beach, when the tide is low. The mine is reportedly haunted by the ghosts of miners who died there, working under great dangerous conditions.

Chapel Porth
St. Agnes, TR5 0NS
Telephone: 01872 552412
Website: www.st-agnes.com/discover/history
Email: godrevy@nationaltrust.org.uk

THE MOLESWORTH ARMS HOTEL

A charming 16th century coach inn, Molesworth Arms is located in the beautiful village of Wadebridge. It was used as a coaching inn for centuries and later became a bed and breakfast and pub. Once known as Wade, Wadebridge changed its name after the bridge was built in the village. It was granted a license for a market in 1312 which makes this village extremely old. There is a haunting that takes place every New Year's Eve. At exactly midnight, a coach is driven into the courtyard of the hotel by a headless coachman. No one knows who he is, but he enjoys returning year after year.

Molesworth Street, Wadebridge, PL27 7DP
Telephone: +44 1208 812055
Website: www.moleswortharms.co.uk

THE WELLINGTON HOTEL

One of the oldest coaching inns in Cornwall, Wellington Hotel goes back to the 17th century. It was known as the Bos Castle Hotel until it changed its name in 1862, after the death of the 'Iron Duke' the Duke of Wellington. It overlooks the harbor of the

Cornish fishing village of Boscastle. There is much history that goes with the Wellington, including reports of three resident ghosts.

A coachman is seen walking through walls along with the ghost of a little girl. An old lady is witnessed walking through walls and closed doors.

The most haunted part of the hotel is reportedly room number nine. It is so prevalent that the hotel's information book has a section dedicated to reported guest experiences, from staying in that room.

One such guest reports "I was lying on the bed when suddenly I felt a really strange sensation and said to myself, 'Oh my God, it's here'." As those words ran through my mind I suddenly felt what can only be described as someone walking up the bed behind me and then a rush of cold air and then total paralysis of my body... I couldn't move I was frozen. I kept thinking if I can just reach the phone I can call my friend but I couldn't. This feeling lasted about 30 seconds and then as quickly as it came... it left me and I felt normal again."

Guests of The Wellington Hotel report seeing the ghosts of a young lady and a man. The man is seen in a frilly shirt with his hair in a ponytail, disappearing through a wall near the hotel's reception room. A young lady who committed suicide is seen as a ghost leaping from the tower that is connected to the main building.

The Wellington Hotel, Boscastle's famous old coaching inn, has more than its fair share of ghostly inhabitants. Some years ago the Hotel's owner, Victor Tobutt was working at the reception desk when the figure of a man drifted silently past him. Looking up he was surprised to see that the man wore leather gaiters and boots, a frock coat and a frilled shirt such as might have been worn by an 18th century coachman. His hair tied back in the old fashioned style, 'There was nothing insubstantial about him.' Victor said, 'he looked remarkably solid.' To his shock, the apparition disappeared through the wall, but when he began to describe to one of his employees what he had seen, the man completed the description for him. He too had seen the ghostly visitor on more than one occasion.

The Wellington Hotel
The Harbour, Boscastle, PL35 0AQ
Telephone: 01840 250202
Website: www.wellingtonhotelboscastle.com
Email: info@wellingtonhotelboscastle.com

LANHYDROCK HOUSE

Lanhydrock is a beautiful country house and estate. There are only two rooms of the original 17th century house that remain since a terrible fire in 1881. The Gallery and Drawing Room are said to be haunted by an odd shaped entity. The building is also haunted by a man who was hanged by Royalists during the Civil War.

Lanhydrock House
Bodmin, PL30 5AD
Telephone: +44 1208 265950

ST NEOT'S CHURCH

"Certain satellites of Satan, names unknown, on the Feast of St John the Apostle – which makes the crime worse – broke into the Parish Church of Poundstock within our Diocese with a host of armed men, during Mass, and before Mass was scarcely completed they furiously entered the Chancel and with swords and staves cut down William Penfound, clerk.

Vestments and other Church Ornaments were desecrated with human blood in contempt of the Creator, in contempt of the Church, to the subversion of ecclesiastical liberty and the disturbance of the peace of the realm. Where will we be safe from crime if the Holy Church, our Mother, the House of God and the Gateway to Heaven is thus deprived of its sanctity?"

-----Bishop of Exeter.

Murdered in 1356, the ghost of William Penfound still haunts the church. His ghost has been seen standing at the church altar and in the graveyard. He is occasionally seen floating to Penfound Manor where he and his family lived for 400 more years.

St. Neot's Church
Cornwall, PL14 6NA
Website: www.stneot.org.uk

ROCHE ROCK

Surrounding the chapel at Roche Rock is Bodmin Moor. A seventeenth century unscrupulous man, Jan Tregeagle's ghost is still heard crying hopelessly, in the chapel.

Though he was a deceitful man, he somehow bribed clergy to bury his body in consecrated ground, after death. After Tregeagle died he came back from the grave to appear as a witness in the court of law. He wanted to testify for himself as he had been charged with wrongfully claiming land, in life. By the end of the trial the court room became cold and chilly, as Tregeagle's ghost appeared in the witness box.

Even though his ghost had appeared, he was still found guilty of fraudulent ownership of the land. According to legend, local clergy took control of the ghost of Tregeagle and set tasks to keep him busy for all eternity. These tasks included emptying Dozmary Pool with a cracked limpet shell. Since he never did what was set before him his spirit will never be at peace.

Location: To the north of St. Austell.

SCARBOROUGH CASTLE

      Scarborough Castle goes back to the 12th century. During the English Civil War it was greatly damaged though it was still used as a prison for a long time. It was also a military barracks until the end of World War I. Piers Gaveston, a favorite of King Edward II, was captured in 1312 at Scarborough Castle. Later taken to Warwick Castle he was held prisoner before execution. Today his headless spirit haunts the ruins of the Castle. He coaxes people to the edge of the castle where he casts them over the cliffs to their deaths. Many visitors feel as if they are being pushed or shoved. Odd laughter is also often heard.

Known as a humorist, Gaveston hid along the castle wall, in the dark. He then would push Barons and Earls who were walking in the late night, along the wall.

During his lifetime from 1307 to 1328, King Edward II was thought to be inept and self-indulgent. His father and his people felt he was influenced by his favorites being Piers Gaveston, Gascon squire and later on, Hugh le Despenser and his son.

Edward II had no sense where politics were concerned. The strongholds that Edward I had taken during his campaigns were lost by his son. During his reign Edward II disappointed his barons who were fearful of Gaveston's influence over him. He was thought to be the king's lover.

Gaveston was executed at Kenilworth in 1312 after the barons captured him. Edward II's wife, Isabella left him, taking his future heir, their son to France. She later returned with her lover in 1326 to dethrone and murder Edward II.

Scarborough Castle
Scarborough Castle Road,
Scarborough, North Yorkshire, YO11 1HY
Telephone: +44 1723 372451
Website: www.scarboroughcastle.co.uk

GODOLPHIN HOUSE

The ghost of the 'white lady' haunts the early Tudor Godolphin House. She walks the path from the house to the chapel. Known as the 'ghost path,' her funeral procession is seen in spirit along that same path. This 'white lady' is believed to be Lady Margaret Godolphin who died giving birth to the first Earl's heir. She reappears on each anniversary of her funeral.

Godolphin Cross
Helston, TR13 9RE
Telephone: +44 1736 763194

HAUNTED WALKS IN CORNWALL

For those who love to go on a good haunted tour or ghost walk, these venues will prove to be some of the best. After all, they are all in the county of Cornwall, known to be the most haunted county in the UK.

The following information regarding some fun ghost adventures is by no means extensive. It is also not promised that the information listed here has not been changed since the writing of this book. It is advisable to contact these venues before venturing out to experience them. Always call ahead and reserve whenever possible.

It is always a good idea to ask information regarding age appropriateness should there be children who may be attending.

1) *Bodmin Jail Paranormal Ghost Walk Nights*

The Bodmin Jail Ghost Walk Nights ---An overnight event. Takes place from 10:30PM-7:00AM.

On arrival a professional psychic medium will greet you. You will learn about psychic and paranormal activity in workshops. This will help you to better understand what will be happening that night. Should you be hungry beforehand, do reserve dinner ahead of time in the onsite restaurant. Tea and coffee will be available during your ghostly overnight stay. Should you think you may be hungry you are encouraged to bring your own snacks and drinks with you. No food will be available for purchase. Alcohol is not allowed.

Wear warm clothing, bring a camera and a flashlight.

At 7:00 AM your visit will end with a full English breakfast to enjoy.

Ghost events are usually held on the first Saturday of each month with more available in October. Call ahead to book and to be sure of availability and correct dates.
Cost: £70

Location/Contact:
Telephone: 01208 76292
Bodmin Jail, Berrycoombe Road, Bodmin PL312NR
Website: www.bodminjail.org/ghost-walk

2)   *Poldark Mine*

> Tours are held April through November at 6:00 PM. Paranormal investigators will join you on your ghost tour.
>
> Discoveries have been made at the Mine. You will hear about past paranormal investigations. You will be given the opportunity to tell of your own ghostly experiences and hear about old miners' superstitions.
>
> Location/Contact:
> Telephone: 01326 573173
> Address: Poldark Mine, Wendron, Helston TR13 0ES
> Website: www.poldark-mine.co.uk/hauntings.html

3)   *Poldark Halloween Ghost Tours*

> During the Halloween season Poldark Mine offers late night ghost tours as well as their earlier tour. You are welcome to take both tours on the same night if you care to, beginning at 6:00PM. Or you may choose to take the later extended ghost tour which will tour the ancient museum building beginning at 11:00PM. This extended tour lasts for two hours ending at 1:00 AM. You will experience being in the mine at midnight by candlelight.

Cost: from £10 to £20

Location/Contact:
Telephone: 01326 573173
Address: Poldark Mine, Wendron, Helston TR13 0ES
Website:www.poldark-mine.co.uk/hauntings.html

4)   *Ghost Walks in Penzance*

Should you take a Penzance Ghost Walk you will be accompanied by a professional guide. It is a fun way to experience a part of Cornwall and learn about its ghostly side. This particular tour has gained a great reputation with many guests returning.

Ghost Walks in Penzance are held on Thursday nights at 8.30 PM from June to September. They are also held on Sunday nights at 8:30 PM in July and August.

Meet outside the Tourist Information Office. It is located between the railroad station and public parking lot.

Cost: £5

Location/Contact:
Telephone: 01736 331206
Address: Station Approach, Penzance TR18 2NF
Website: www.ghosthunting.org.uk

5)   *Ghost Walks in St Ives*

A fun engaging tour, many return for a second walk. You will be accompanied by an experienced guide. St. Ive's ghostly past will be experienced first- hand.

Ghost Tours in St Ives are held on:

• May-October: Tuesday nights at 8.30pm
• June-August: Tuesday and Wednesday nights at 8.30pm
• August: There are some later ghost tours at 10:15pm during the peak of the month.

The St Ives Ghost Tours all start from outside the Tourist Information Office which is in the town.

Cost: £5

Location/Contact:
Telephone: 01736 331206
Address: The Guildhall, Street-An-Pol, St. Ives TR26 2DS
Website:
http://sites.google.com/site/ghosthuntingcornwall/p enzanceghostwalks

6)   *Ghost Tours at Pengersick Castle*

Seen on TV's Most Haunted show, this is a privately owned castle. Many experience more ghosts and hauntings here than most other locations.

Very often, tours at Pengersick Castle run on Saturday evenings. Call ahead to enquire.

Halloween Ghost Tours are also usually available at Pengersick Castle. Call ahead to book.

Location/Contact:
Telephone: 01736 762579
Address: Pengersick Castle, Praa Sands TR20 9SJ
Website: http://ghosthunting.cornwall

7)   *Ghost Walks in Newquay*

Summer months and Halloween season brings fun ghosts walks in Newquay. Located on the north coast of Cornwall, you will join ghost guide Shawn Curnow.

Tour begins at the Newquay Tourist Information Center, on Marcus Hill. 8:00 PM is start time on Tuesday and Thursday evenings during the summer. The Ghost Walks in Newquay will run approximately 90 minutes.

Location/Contact:
Address: Newquay Tourist Information Center, Marcus Hill, Newquay TR7/1BD
Website:
http://encounterswithspirit.webs.com/events.htm

8) <u>*Ghost Walks on the Isles of Scilly*</u>

So many ghosts are seen and heard throughout the Isles of Scilly, 26 miles off the coast of Cornwall. Known for its history of smugglers and shipwrecks, many ghosts remain.

Ghost walks take place on occasion. They are organized by George Teidman. They usually begin at the Bell Rock Hotel and end at the Star Hotel, St. Mary's. There is no set schedule for these walks. They usually last about 2 ½ hours

Cost: £5

Location/Contact:
Website:
www.scilly.gov.uk/events/event.htm?pk_events=861

9) <u>*Ghost Tours at Pendennis Castle*</u>

Haunted Halloween at Pendennis Castle is fun entertainment for the whole family. Booking is a must as it is a very popular tour. There are three tours each day: 11:00AM, 1:30PM, and 3:00PM. Tours are available the entire week before Halloween, right up to the day. Do confirm ahead of time as the dates do change yearly.

Cost: £2.90/child, £5.40/adult, £14.30/family.

Also offered are adults only ghost tours. They run two nights in the week prior to Halloween, as well. Two tours are usually available: 7:30PM and 9:30PM.

Cost: £12

Location/Contact:
Telephone: 01326 316594
Address: Pendennis Castle, Pendennis Headland, Falmouth TR11 4LP
Website: www.english-heritage.org.uk

10) *Lantern Ghost Storywalk*

If you have not made any reservations ahead of time for a fun ghost walk, you will be happy to know that you can just show up for this one. The walk takes place around St. Ives and lasts about 45 minutes. You are also welcome to book ahead for a private walk. Start times do change depending on the time of year. Contact Shanty Baba at the phone number on the website.

Cost: £5 adults, Under 14s £3. No booking required.

Location/Contact:
The walks leave from Westcott's Quay, which is located 120m behind the RNLI Lifeboat House, along the seawall heading towards the station, by the St Ives Arts Club.

Website: www.lanternghoststorywalk.com

ABOUT THE AUTHOR

Bonnie has been a business owner for many years. As a dressmaker and graduate of Maison Sapho School of Dressmaking in New York City, she was the owner of a home-based business while raising her children. Bonnie has also earned a degree in social work.

Raised a United Methodist minister's daughter, Bonnie is often called a 'PK,' short for 'Preacher's Kid.' A church organist in the past, she also directed adult and children's choirs, brass ensembles, and hand bell choirs. She is an extensively trained soprano and has performed a solo concert at the Crystal Cathedral in California, home church of the Rev. Robert Schuller. In addition, Bonnie is a Christian recording artist, an accomplished cellist and flutist, and has taught many children to play the piano.

For several years Bonnie has written for many publications, most recently the Examiner. As a certified Reiki Master she also maintains a professional practice, Reiki Health and Healing .

In addition, Bonnie is the owner and creator of the most haunted tour in Williamsburg, Virginia, USA. Having personally experienced many ghosts, she has created a one-of-a-kind tour based on fully researched ghost stories.

Bonnie resides in Williamsburg, Virginia with husband Tom Florek, daughter Julie Eynard, son Eric Redmond II, and grandchildren Jaycee Redmond and Eric Redmond III.

ABOUT SPOOKS AND LEGENDS

HAUNTED TOURS, LLC

From start to finish, a *Spooks and Legends Haunted Tour* is engaging, fun for all and most importantly, based on fully researched ghost stories and reported sightings. This tour is unique and has become the #1 tour of choice in Williamsburg, Virginia, USA, in just a few short years. Williamsburg is a very haunted town, yet most tours do not fully embrace that truth.

Spooks and Legends tours are led by an 18th century costumed 'ghost guide' who becomes the character of a real person who lived in town during the Revolution. As guests become engaged they forget that the guide is a real living person. It is a very realistic tour with other town characters often meeting the tour group along the way, as they walk the eerie streets of the old haunted town.

Guests have attended from all over the world including the Netherlands, England, India, Canada, France, Russia, and Germany. *Spooks and Legends'* excellent Trip Advisor reviews say it all.

Character Fred Vick is a real asset to *Spooks and Legends Haunted Tours*, playing several different ghost characters. As 'Peter,' the town jailer and church organist, his interactions with 'Catherine Rathell' prove to be quite interesting. He stops for a few moments to greet guests on his way to yet another town tavern, while also searching for some of his convicted jail escapees.

New to our tours are child characters 'Elizabeth and James Geddy,' played by Jaycee Redmond and Eric Redmond, III. This is especially exciting for our younger guests. These 18th century children give the tour a personal touch for all ages.

For more information or to attend an ever-popular *Spooks and Legends Tour*, please go to our website: *www.spooksandlegends.com or* contact Bonnie directly at: *spooksandlegends@aol.com* / *1-757-784-6213*. We look forward to meeting you and giving you an experience of a lifetime.

** If you would like to have your venue featured in one of Bonnie's up-coming books, submit information regarding your ghost tour, haunted walk, or other ghostly location. Any and all information will be considered for one of her two new book series *Totally Haunted USA* or *Totally Haunted UK*. Please contact her by email or phone. She will choose the most interesting, most haunted submissions to include in her upcoming books. Those who contribute will get special recognition for their venue.

www.spooksandlegends.com
spooksandlegends@aol.com

757-784-6213

Don't forget to LIKE us on Facebook

Please review this book on Amazon.com and Amazon.uk. Should you write a book I will be happy to read it and write a review for you as well. Thank you so much. *BOO!*